W9-AOT-997

TEXAS TEST PREP

Writing Workbook

STAAR Writing

Grade 6

© 2012 by Test Master Press

All rights reserved. No part of this book may be reproduced or transmitted in any form or by any means, electronic, mechanical, photocopying, recording, or otherwise without prior written permission.

ISBN 978-1468023749

CONTENTS

INTRODUCTION
For Parents, Teachers, and Tutors

About the Book

This book is designed to help students develop both their reading comprehension and their writing skills. The skills learned in this book will help students succeed on the STAAR Reading test and the STAAR Writing test.

Part 1: Reading and Writing Mini-Tests

Part 1 of this book has reading and writing mini-tests. These mini-tests offer practice providing written answers to reading comprehension questions. Students will read and respond to a wide range of passages and answer all types of short-response and essay questions. Part 1 also includes Core Writing Skills Practice exercises. Each exercise is focused on one core writing skill that grade 6 students are expected to have.

Part 2: Responding to Literature

Part 2 of this book provides guided practice for writing essays based on passages. The planning process followed for each task will help students develop the skills to write clear, focused, and well-written essays. The hints provided with the writing tasks are focused on the attributes that teachers and scorers look for in student writing, and will help students produce writing that will score well on tests.

Part 3: Guided Writing Tasks

Part 3 of this book provides guided practice for all the common writing tasks that grade 6 students will encounter. Students will have practice planning and writing stories, personal narratives, essays, and persuasive texts. The hints provided with the writing tasks will help student produce writing with the key attributes expected of each type of writing. As well as developing and improving general writing skills, this section will prepare students for the writing prompts on the STAAR Writing test taken by all grade 7 students.

Part 1
Reading and Writing
Mini-Tests

INTRODUCTION
For Parents, Teachers, and Tutors

Reading and Writing Skills

Students in grade 6 develop both their reading and writing skills. This section of the book will help students improve their reading comprehension skills and their writing skills. Students will practice understanding and responding to a wide range of passage types. Students will also practice answering many different types of short-response questions.

About the Reading and Writing Mini-Tests

This section of the workbook contains four mini-tests. Each mini-test has five short passages. Each passage is followed by two questions. Students should answer each question by writing their response on the lines. The last passage in each mini-test also has a longer essay question.

This section of the book provides students with the opportunity to practice their reading and writing skills using short passages. Students can focus on one passage and a small set of questions at a time. This will build confidence and help students become familiar with answering short-response questions.

This section of the book is also an effective way for students to build up to answering the longer essay questions in Part 2 of this book.

 ## Developing Core Writing Skills

Each mini-test also includes Core Writing Skills Practice exercises. Each exercise focuses on one core writing skill that grade 6 students need to develop. Some of these exercises require students to write a longer piece of writing such as a research report, a short story, or a letter. These exercises have the icon above next to them. Students should write or type their responses on a separate piece of paper.

Hints

Some of the questions in this section of the book include hints. These will guide students on how to answer the question, provide extra information that will help students answer the question correctly, or define a key term used in the question. The hints are based on what teachers and scorers look for in answers, and will help students learn to answer questions so they receive maximum points.

Reading and Writing

Mini-Test 1

Instructions

Read each passage. Complete the exercise under each passage. Some of the exercises have a notepad icon next to them. Complete these exercises by writing or typing your answer on a separate sheet of paper.

Then complete the questions on the next page. Read each question carefully. Then write your answer in the space provided.

Mozart

Mozart is a famous German composer of the classical era. He is also known as Wolfgang Amadeus Mozart. He has composed over 600 pieces of classical music. These include works for the piano and violin, as well as whole operas.

Mozart began composing at the age of 5. At this time, he wrote small pieces for his father. He continued to learn and write music all through his youth. When he was 17, he worked as a court musician in Austria. He was given the opportunity to write a range of musical pieces. Mozart left Austria in search of better work, and lived in Paris for over a year. During this time, he was unable to find work, but he still continued writing music. He then moved to Vienna. Mozart wrote most of his best-known work while living in Vienna. He died at the age of 35 in 1791.

CORE WRITING SKILLS PRACTICE
WRITE A RESEARCH REPORT

Mozart was one famous composer during the classical era. Another famous composer was Ludwig van Beethoven. Research and write a short report about Ludwig van Beethoven. Use the questions below to guide your research.

Where and when was Beethoven born?

Where did Beethoven live during his life?

What music did Beethoven write?

What are some of Beethoven's best-known works?

What influence did Beethoven's music have?

1   Mozart can be described as gifted. Give **two** details that show that Mozart was gifted.

1. _____

   _____

2. _____

   _____

2   Complete the chart below by describing **two** places that Mozart lived after Austria and what he did in each place.

Place	Details
Austria	Worked as a court musician

Clowns

Mickey didn't like clowns. When his family told him that he would be going to the circus, he was excited. He knew there would be lions, camels, and a trapeze artist. Then he remembered that there would also be clowns. He became very nervous.

"Don't worry," said his father. "You'll be fine. Your mother and I will be with you."

Mickey felt a little better and decided to go. He took his seat in the front row of the audience. The trapeze artists performed first, and Mickey was amazed by their skill. After a short break, it was time for the clowns. As the clowns came out onto the stage, Mickey froze. He thought about running off, even though he wasn't really sure what he was afraid of. But he sat quietly in his seat reminding himself over and over that there was nothing to fear.

Gradually, his feelings of fear faded away. He started to smile as the clowns pranced around. By the time the performance was over, Mickey was giggling along with everyone else in the audience.

©Abby Norling-Ruggles

1   What is Mickey's main problem? How does he overcome his problem?

_____

_____

_____

_____

_____

2   In the last paragraph, what does the word "pranced" suggest about the clowns?

Hint   This question is asking you to think about more than just the dictionary meaning of the word. Think about what image it creates, or how it makes you feel.

_____

_____

_____

_____

Raindrops

It is a popular belief that rain falls in droplets shaped like teardrops. Raindrops are often drawn to look this way. If you've ever watched a weather report on the news, you might have seen symbols representing rainfall. The raindrops are often shown as if they are teardrops. This is a nice idea, but not a practical one.

Raindrops are actually spherical rather than teardrop-shaped. This is a common property of falling liquid. Raindrops also change shape depending on how they are falling. If they are falling fast, the bottom might be pushed up. The top will then stay rounded, but the bottom will be pushed flat. The shape is a little like the top of a mushroom.

1   What is the main purpose of the diagram?

Hint   To answer this question, you should explain what the diagram shows and how it relates to the information in the passage.

_____

_____

_____

_____

2   Compare the actual shape of raindrops with the shape that many people think they are.

_____

_____

_____

_____

Dearest Donna

One year together, one year of bliss,
You brighten my days with your tender kiss.
I hope that you'll be my sweet valentine,
And say that you will always be mine.

In the future we may well get married,
On the wings of love we'll be carried.
As we grow old as one and together,
Side by side as partners forever.

CORE WRITING SKILLS PRACTICE
WRITE A POEM

This poem is a rhyming poem. One common rhyme pattern is to have the second and fourth lines of a poem rhyme. Here is an example of this rhyme pattern:

It was a dark and stormy night.
There was a huge thunder crash.
Into my room and under my bed,
the poor little cat did dash.

Choose a pair of rhyming words from the list below. Use the words to write a poem with four lines where the second and fourth lines rhyme.

street	beat	eat	seat	sweet
meet	greet	treat	sleet	cheat

1   Describe the rhyme pattern of the poem "Dearest Donna."

_____

_____

_____

_____

2   Who is the speaker addressing the poem to? Explain how you can tell.

Hint   Think about how the speaker uses the words "you" and "we" in the poem. The title of the poem is also important.

_____

_____

_____

Penny's Powers

Penny was a beautiful princess. She lived in a tall towering castle that almost reached the clouds. What people didn't know was that she had special super wishing powers. But Penny often failed to use them because she had everything she had ever wanted. She had no need to wish for food, or pretty things, or happy times. Every day was pleasant for Penny.

One day, a homeless man visited her and asked for help. Penny used her powers to give him money, a cozy home, and fresh food. Penny was shocked by how pleased the man was. She had never realized how lucky she was. From that day forward, she decided to use her powers to help as many people as she could.

CORE WRITING SKILLS PRACTICE

Imagine that you have special wishing powers. What is the first wish you would make? Explain why you would make that wish.

_____

_____

_____

_____

_____

_____

_____

1 How can you tell that the events in the passage could not really happen?

Hint The events in the passage are made-up and could not happen in real life. Explain how you can tell this.

_____

_____

_____

_____

2 Identify the hyperbole in the first paragraph and explain why the author used it.

Hint Hyperbole is a literary technique where exaggeration is used to make a point or emphasize the qualities of something.

_____

_____

_____

_____

3   How does Penny change in the passage? What causes Penny to change?
Use details from the passage in your answer.

> **Hint**   To answer this question, start by describing what Penny is like at the start of the passage. Then describe what makes her change. Finish by explaining how she has changed.

_____

_____

_____

_____

_____

_____

_____

_____

Reading and Writing

Mini-Test 2

Instructions

Read each passage. Complete the exercise under each passage. Some of the exercises have a notepad icon next to them. Complete these exercises by writing or typing your answer on a separate sheet of paper.

Then complete the questions on the next page. Read each question carefully. Then write your answer in the space provided.

Something Special

Toby had played basketball for the school since he was eleven. When he reached sixteen, he was dropped from the team because his coach said he was too short. Toby was upset, but his father told him not to give up. He told him to keep playing and enjoying the game.

Toby played on the weekend with his friends. After school, he played by himself. Without anyone else to play with, he spent a lot of time learning ball skills. He enjoyed learning to do new things with the ball. But he missed playing in real games and being part of a team.

When they moved the following year, Toby trained with his new school team. His coach was impressed with his ball skills. Toby was delighted to be selected for the team. He later became the star player for his new team.

CORE WRITING SKILLS PRACTICE
WRITE A PERSUASIVE LETTER

Imagine that you are Toby. You have just been dropped from the team and want to write a letter to your coach. You want to persuade your coach to let you play on the team again. List three reasons your coach should let you play below. Then write a persuasive letter to your coach using these reasons.

1. _____

_____

2. _____

_____

3. _____

_____

1   Use information from the passage to complete the table below.

Ways that Toby Keeps Playing Basketball After He is Dropped from the School Team
1)
2)

2   How does Toby being dropped from the school team lead to his later success?

Hint   This question is asking you about cause and effect. What happens because Toby is dropped from the team? How does what happens help him in the end?

_____

_____

_____

_____

Brain Size

Did you know that the common ant has the largest brain in relation to its size? The brain of an ant is 6 percent of its total body weight. The average human brain is just over 2 percent of a person's body weight.

A single ant brain has a fraction of the ability of a human one. But a colony of ants may have just as much ability. An average nest has 40,000 ants. In total, these ants would have about the same number of brain cells as a person.

CORE WRITING SKILLS PRACTICE

Ants often work together. To do this, they have to communicate with each other. Research and write a short description of how ants communicate.

_____

_____

_____

_____

_____

_____

_____

_____

1   Why do you think the author starts the passage with a question?

> **Hint**   To answer this question, think about the author's purpose. How does starting with a question affect readers?

_____

_____

_____

_____

2   Describe **two** facts given about ants.

> **Hint**   A fact is something that can be proven to be true.

1. _____

_____

2. _____

_____

Mosquitoes

It is well known that mosquitoes carry disease. But did you know that only females bite humans? Male mosquitoes only bite plants and greenery. Both genders carry over 100 separate diseases. It is the female of the species though, that passes these diseases onto members of the human race.

It was only in 1877 that British doctor Patrick Manson first discovered that mosquitoes could be very dangerous creatures.

CORE WRITING SKILLS PRACTICE

There are many diseases that are spread by mosquitoes. Use the Internet to find out the names of some diseases that are passed onto people by mosquitoes. Complete the list below by adding four more diseases that are spread by mosquitoes.

1. Malaria

2. _____

3. _____

4. _____

5. _____

1   If the author added another sentence to the end of the article, what do you think it would describe?

_____

_____

_____

_____

_____

2   Describe **one** way that male and female mosquitoes are similar. Describe **one** way that male and female mosquitoes are different.

Hint   Make sure you use information from the passage when identifying similarities and differences.

_____

_____

_____

_____

The Olympics

The Olympics are a global sporting event. They feature both outdoor and indoor sports. They are watched and enjoyed by people all over the world. They are an important event because they bring people from all countries together.

They are held in both a summer and winter format. The Winter Olympics and Summer Olympics are both held every 4 years. The first modern Olympics were held in 1896. Many nations compete in each Olympic event. A different country hosts the games each time. The city of London in the United Kingdom is the host of the 2012 Olympics.

Year	Held
2012	London, United Kingdom
2008	Beijing, China
2004	Athens, Greece
2000	Sydney, Australia
1996	Atlanta, United States
1992	Barcelona, Spain

CORE WRITING SKILLS PRACTICE
WRITE A RESEARCH REPORT

Choose one Olympic athlete from the list below. Research and write a report on that athlete. Include what sport they competed in, which Olympic Games they competed at, and their main achievements.

Michael Phelps
Usain Bolt
Carl Lewis
Muhammad Ali
Babe Didrickson
Mary Lou Retton

1   List **one** fact and **one** opinion given about the Olympics.

Hint   A fact is a statement that can be proven to be true. An opinion is a statement that cannot be proven to be true.

Fact: _____

_____

Opinion: _____

_____

2   Why do you think the Olympics is so popular all around the world?

Hint   This question is asking for your personal opinion. You can use details in the passage in your answer. You can also use your own knowledge and ideas.

_____

_____

_____

_____

The Light

Christopher woke up late one evening. He was drawn to a light shining in through his window. He hurried downstairs and out into the back garden. Something bright and dazzling glimmered in the sky above him.

Christopher shielded his eyes as it moved towards him. It finally rested before him on the grass. As he stepped backwards, a door opened. A strange green outstretched arm welcomed him aboard. He paused, before stepping forward into the light.

CORE WRITING SKILLS PRACTICE

The story is written from third person point of view. Write a description of the events from the story from Christopher's point of view.

_____

_____

_____

_____

_____

_____

_____

_____

1   How does the author help the reader imagine the light?

Hint   Focus on the words and phrases the author uses to describe the light. List these words and phrases in your answer and explain their impact.

_____

_____

_____

_____

2   Do you think Christopher feels curious or afraid at the end of the passage? Use details from the passage to support your answer.

_____

_____

_____

_____

3   What do you think the light is? What do you think happens next in the passage? Use details from the passage in your answer.

Hint

This question is asking you to draw a conclusion about what the light is. Use the details given in the passage to draw your conclusion. Then make a prediction about what happens to Christopher next.

_____

_____

_____

_____

_____

_____

_____

_____

Reading and Writing

Mini-Test 3

Instructions

Read each passage. Complete the exercise under each passage. Some of the exercises have a notepad icon next to them. Complete these exercises by writing or typing your answer on a separate sheet of paper.

Then complete the questions on the next page. Read each question carefully. Then write your answer in the space provided.

Peace and Not War

Terry was watching football in the lounge room, when his younger brother Mark walked in and changed the channel. Mark was determined to watch his favorite cartoon. They fought over the remote control. Then they started arguing.

"I hate watching football," Mark yelled.

"I hate watching cartoons," Terry yelled back.

Their voices got louder and louder. The lounge room began to sound like a zoo. Their mother came in from the kitchen. Without saying anything, she picked up the remote and turned off the television.

"If you can't watch the television nicely, then you can't watch it at all," she said.

CORE WRITING SKILLS PRACTICE

Think of an argument you have had with someone. Describe who you argued with and what you argued about.

_____

_____

_____

_____

_____

_____

1   Why do Mark and Terry fight? Use details from the passage in your answer.

Hint   To answer this question, do not just write that they fight over the television. Explain why they fight over the television.

_____

_____

_____

_____

2   The author says that the lounge room "began to sound like a zoo." Explain what the author means by this.

_____

_____

_____

_____

The Dodo

The dodo was a species of flightless bird that became extinct. It lived on the island of Mauritius. It lived in an environment free from ground-based predators. When humans arrived on the island, they brought with them many ground-based animals. These included rats, pigs, and dogs. These animals ate dodo's eggs from their nests. The eggs were easy to get to because the nests were on the ground. Humans also hunted dodos for their meat. Humans also destroyed the dodo's forest habitats. The number of dodos decreased until they became extinct.

The dodo will always be remembered because it led to a common phrase. The slang phrase "as dead as a dodo" is used to describe something that is gone forever or definitely dead.

CORE WRITING SKILLS PRACTICE
WRITE A RESEARCH REPORT

The dodo is one animal that has become extinct, but it is not the only one. Choose one extinct animal from the list below. Use the Internet to find out why the animal became extinct. Then write a report describing your findings.

mammoth
mastodon
megalodon
saber-toothed cat
Tasmanian tiger

1   Explain what common phrase refers to the dodo and describe what the phrase means.

Hint   This question is asking you to summarize specific information given in the passage. Make sure you use your own words when writing your answer.

_____

_____

_____

_____

_____

2   Give **two** reasons that dodos became extinct.

1. _____

2. _____

_____

Letter to the Editor

Dear Editor,

I am worried that our town park does not look as nice as it once did. It is not as well-cared for and is not cleaned as often. There are food wrappers, cans, and even broken glass lying around. I've noticed that there is a lot of graffiti appearing too.

I think that something must be done about this! It is no longer a lovely place to spend the afternoon. It is not even a safe place to play with all the trash lying around. The people of our town need to demand that something be done about this.

Yours with hope,

Evan

CORE WRITING SKILLS PRACTICE

Think about the problem that Evan is describing. How do you think the problem could be solved? Write a paragraph describing your solution to the problem.

_____

_____

_____

_____

_____

_____

1   Complete the web below using information from the article.

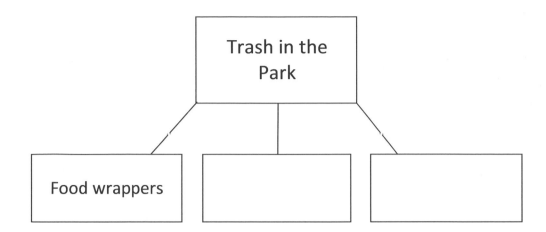

2   Evan argues that the town park does not look as nice as it once did. How do you think Evan could make this argument more convincing?

   Think about what information Evan could include to help readers better understand what the park looks like now, or how the park has changed.

_____

_____

_____

_____

_____

Tom's Time Machine

Tom had spent almost a decade designing and building his time machine. He had spent countless hours in his laboratory. After he developed it, he had done many experiments sending small objects through time. And now, after all his hard work, it was finally time to test it for himself. He entered the time machine, and began to type into the computer.

Tom had always wanted to go back to the dinosaur age. He set the time to 80 million years ago. As the machine went dark and began to shake, he knew he was on his way deep into the unknown. He was scared, but thrilled with the idea that he might see a real dinosaur. He just hoped to himself that the first one he saw was a friendly one.

CORE WRITING SKILLS PRACTICE
WRITE A SHORT STORY

If you had a time machine, what time would you travel to? It could be a time far in the past like Tom, a time more recently in the past, or a time in the future. Imagine you have traveled to that time. Write a story describing your journey. Answer the questions below to help plan your story. Then write your story.

What time would you travel to?

_____

What would you do once you arrived?

_____

What would the past or future look like?

_____

1   Circle the word below that best describes Tom. Then explain why you chose that word.

adventurous   **brave**   **determined**

_____

_____

_____

_____

2   What genre is the passage? Explain how you can tell.

> **Hint**   Genre refers to the category a work of literature falls into. Common genres include mystery, fantasy, horror, adventure, science fiction, and historical fiction.

_____

_____

_____

_____

Creature Comforts

Fred the farmer loved his job. He enjoyed nothing more than waking up at sunrise to feed and tend to his animals. He would even sing to them as he visited them in the morning. Even during the cold days of winter, he never once complained. He just put on thick socks and an extra coat and went out into the freezing cold air. The wind whipped around him and tried to annoy him. But Fred just focused on his tasks.

When the summer sun rose high in the sky and the day became very hot, he still loved working hard. He was always pleased knowing that he was making his animals happy and comfortable. Although they couldn't speak, Fred knew that his animals were happy with their life on his farm.

CORE WRITING SKILLS PRACTICE

The passage describes how Fred loves being a farmer. Do you think you would enjoy being a farmer? Explain why or why not.

_____

_____

_____

_____

_____

_____

_____

1   What is the main theme of the passage?

> **Hint**   The theme of a passage is the idea it expresses, or a lesson it aims to teach.

_____

_____

_____

_____

2   Identify the personification used in the first paragraph. Then explain why the author used it.

> **Hint**   Personification is a literary technique where objects are given human qualities, or described as if they are human.

_____

_____

_____

_____

3   What do you think matters most to Fred? Use details from the passage to
support your answer.

Hint   Start by stating what you think matters most to Fred. Then
explain why you think this. Use two or three details from the
passage to support your answer.

_____

_____

_____

_____

_____

_____

_____

_____

_____

Reading and Writing

Mini-Test 4

Instructions

Read each passage. Complete the exercise under each passage. Some of the exercises have a notepad icon next to them. Complete these exercises by writing or typing your answer on a separate sheet of paper.

Then complete the questions on the next page. Read each question carefully. Then write your answer in the space provided.

Sugar

Did you know that sugar is a type of crystal? The crystal is edible. It is made out of a fructose molecule and a glucose molecule bonded together to form tiny crystals. If you looked at one crystal through a microscope, it would be shaped like a cube. It can form large crystals or fine crystals. Large crystals can be crushed or ground down to make finer crystals.

Under normal conditions, the molecules of sugar crystallize. When heated without water, the sugar crystals begin to melt. This process is called caramelization. This process is often used to make sweets such as toffees and syrups.

CORE WRITING SKILLS PRACTICE
WRITE A RECIPE

Sugar is used to make many things. The list below describes some common desserts that are made using sugar. Choose one of the desserts and research how it is made. Then write your own recipe describing how to make it.

caramel apples
meringue
candied almonds
caramel popcorn
toffee
peanut brittle

1   Describe **two** things you learned about sugar.

Hint   Use the inforrmation in the passage to answer this question. But make sure you write your answer in your own words.

1. _____

_____

2. _____

_____

2   What would you do if you wanted sugar to undergo caramelization?

_____

_____

_____

_____

Herbal Tea

1. Add water to a kettle and wait until it has boiled.

2. Rinse the cup with boiling water to warm it up.

3. Place a tea bag and a teaspoon or two of sugar (if required) in the cup.

4. Add the water and allow to sit for 30 seconds. You can let it sit for longer if you like your tea stronger.

5. Use a spoon to squeeze the tea bag. Then remove and stir the liquid.

6. If you like, you can also add a dash of milk or cream.

If you are making tea for several people, follow the same steps but use a teapot instead of a cup.

CORE WRITING SKILLS PRACTICE	
There are different types of herbal teas. Research the benefits of different types of teas. Use the information to complete the table below.	
Type of Tea	**Main Benefit**
Green tea	Lowers cholesterol
Peppermint tea	
Chamomile tea	

1   What is the main purpose of the passage?

Hint

When answering questions like this, you should state the general purpose of the passage. You should also support your answer by explaining how you can tell what the purpose is.

_____

_____

_____

_____

_____

2   Describe **two** actions in the process of making tea that are optional.

1. _____

_____

2. _____

_____

A Day in the Life

Jenny was so proud of her father. He was a local police officer. Jenny's father took great pride in protecting people and keeping them safe. Jenny loved it when her father came home in the evening. He would talk about everything that happened that day.

Sometimes he would tell how he tracked down a thief. Other times, he would describe how he directed traffic after an accident. Another day, he might tell how he pulled over people who were speeding. Some days, all he did was sit at his desk and do paperwork.

No matter what he told her, Jenny was always impressed. When she slept at night, Jenny would dream that one day she would be like her father.

CORE WRITING SKILLS PRACTICE
WRITE A SHORT STORY

Imagine that something exciting happens to Jenny's father the next time he goes to work. Write a short story describing the event. Answer the questions below to help plan your story. Then write your story.

What exciting event happens to Jenny's father?

_____

What does Jenny's father do?

_____

What happens in the end?

_____

1   Complete the web below using information from the passage.

   The center of the web tells you what the web is listing. Make sure you only complete the web with details that are included in the passage.

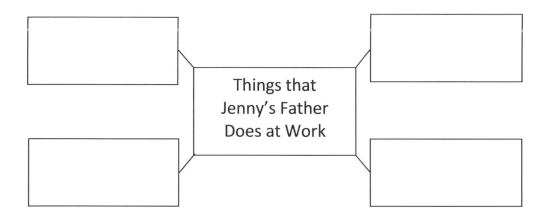

2   Explain why "A Day in the Life" is a suitable title for the passage.

_____

_____

_____

_____

_____

Silver

Silver is a shiny metal. It is the best conductor of both heat and electricity. Even though it conducts electricity well, silver is not often used in wiring. Copper is used in wiring because it is far cheaper to buy. Silver is also the most reflective of all the metals. It is used in mirrors and other reflective coatings. It is also used in photographic film. Another use is in solar panels and electronic devices such as mobile phones.

Silver is often used to make jewelry, cutlery, and items like serving plates. Silver can even be used to sterilize water. This has been known for a very long time. The Persian king Cyrus the Great had his water supply boiled and sealed in silver vessels.

Silver is also used to make coins and medals. Quarters, dimes, and nickels are not made from silver, but investors can buy coins made of silver.

Silver Use in 2011

Use of Silver	Percent Used
Photography	24%
Jewelry	20%
Silverware	12%
Coins and Medals	3%
Industrial Uses (such as solar panels and mobile phones)	40%

1   How is the information in the table important to the passage?

Hint   In your answer, describe what information is given in the table and how it relates to or expands on the information in the passage.

_____

_____

_____

_____

2   Even though silver is a good conductor of electricity, it is rarely used in wiring. Explain why.

_____

_____

_____

_____

Camels

Camels can survive for long periods of time without drinking water. The camel's hump is a big help with this. But it does not actually store water. It stores fat. The fat is used as a source of energy. Camels do store water. They store it in their bodies and in their blood.

Camels can go longer than 7 days without drinking. When they do find water, they can take a lot in. They are able to consume over 50 gallons of water at a time! These features allow them to survive in the desert. Camels were once found in North America. They are now mainly found in the deserts of the African and Arabian regions.

CORE WRITING SKILLS PRACTICE
WRITE A RESEARCH REPORT

There are many other plants and animals that are suited to desert conditions. Choose one of the plants or animals listed below. Research what features the plant or animal has that help it survive in the desert. Then write a report describing what you learned.

rattlesnake
Gila monster
prickly pear
saguaro cactus

1   How does a camel's hump help it survive?

_____

_____

_____

2   Which details from the passage did you find most interesting?

Hint   This question is asking for your personal opinion. As well as describing what you found most interesting, make sure you also briefly explain why.

_____

_____

_____

_____

3   What features allow camels to survive in deserts? Use details from the passage in your answer.

Hint   Focus on how the features of camels help them overcome the main problems of living in deserts.

_____

_____

_____

_____

_____

_____

_____

_____

_____

_____

_____

_____

_____

_____

_____

_____

_____

Part 2
Responding to Literature

INTRODUCTION
For Parents, Teachers, and Tutors

Responding to Literature

Students in grade 6 will often be asked to respond to literature. In these tasks, students read a passage and then answer an essay question based on the passage. The essay question might require students to summarize the passage, analyze the passage, or to apply the passage to their own lives. The writing tasks in this section of the book will help students improve their reading comprehension skills and their writing skills.

This section of the book contains five writing tasks. Each writing task has a passage for students to read and is followed by an essay question based on the passage.

Planning

Planning is the key to having students produce writing that is clear, focused, and effective. For each writing task, students should follow the instructions for planning their writing and complete the planning page before they start writing their essay. Students should then write an essay of between 1 and 2 pages.

Hints

Each writing task includes a hint. Each hint is designed to have students focus on one area that will help them achieve good results in written tasks. After completing all five tasks, students will have developed key skills that will help ensure they score well on future writing tasks.

Responding to Literature

About the Writing Tasks

In these writing tasks, you will first read a passage. Then you will write an essay based on the passage you have read. You should use information from the passage in your answer.

Before you start writing, use the planning page to plan your writing. Follow the steps on the next page to plan your writing.

Plan Your Writing

Before you start writing, plan what you are going to write.

Step 1
Start by reading the question carefully. Focus on what the question is asking you to write about.

Step 2
Fill in the first box by writing a short summary of what you are going to write about. Make sure what you are going to write about matches what the question is asking you to do.

Step 3
When writing an essay based on a passage, it is important to include details from the passage. Fill in the second box by listing the facts, details, or examples from the passage that you are going to use in your essay.

Step 4
Fill in the third box by writing a plan of what you are going to write. Write down the main points you want to make, and the order you are going to cover them. Make sure you include an introduction and a conclusion.

Step 5
Start writing! Follow your plan as you write.

Step 6
After you have finished, check your work. Check your work for spelling, grammar, punctuation, and capitalization.

Responding to Literature – Writing Task 1

Directions: Read the passage below. Then answer the question that follows.

Playing a Musical Instrument

Playing a musical instrument is a popular pastime for all age ranges. Young or old, it is lots of fun to play a musical instrument. There are many different types to choose from including guitar, piano, trumpet, and saxophone.

Making a Choice

First, you need to choose a musical instrument that you would like to learn how to play. Here are some things you should think about:

- the cost of the instrument
- how easy or difficult the instrument is to learn
- whether there is a teacher available to help you learn it
- what opportunities there will be to play it

Getting Your Gear

Now you have chosen your instrument, you need to buy it. If it is expensive, you might like to borrow it instead. That way, you can make sure it is the right choice before spending a lot of money.

Some schools will lend students instruments. Or perhaps you can look in your local paper or online for a secondhand instrument, which are usually much cheaper.

Getting Ready to Learn

After you have your instrument, you should then create a learning plan. This might involve private lessons with a music teacher or going to music classes. Some people choose to learn on their own. You can use books, movies, web sites, or you can even watch videos online.

To learn quickly, your plan may include a variety of learning methods. Make sure that you attend every lesson or study your books regularly. Also, be sure to practice what you have learned as this is the best way to develop your new skill.

Making Music

Once you have learned enough to play a song, you should start playing for people. It is a good idea to start with your family or friends. Or you might play for your music class. Once you become confident, you can then play for larger groups of people.

Keep Going

To become a good musician, you have to keep playing. Keep learning as much as you can and practice often. Challenge yourself to learn more difficult songs as well. As you learn more, you will become better and better. Some people even become good enough to play music as a career.

1   If you were going to play a musical instrument, what type would you choose and why? What would you do to learn to play? Use details from the passage in your answer.

In your answer, be sure to

• describe what musical instrument you would choose and why
• describe how you would learn to play
• use details from the passage in your answer
• write an answer of between 1 and 2 pages

Hint

The passage gives advice on how to choose a musical instrument, and describes how readers can learn to play. To answer this question, you should write about how you would use the information in a real situation. You should refer to the advice given in the passage. However, you do not have to use all the advice. An essay that gets full marks will not just repeat all the advice given in the passage. To get full marks, you should show that you are analyzing the advice and deciding for yourself whether to take it. You should apply it to your particular situation. If you are going to follow a certain piece of advice, be sure to clearly explain why. You can also add some of your own ideas. For example, you might have other ideas on what to consider when choosing a musical instrument, or other ideas on how you could learn to play.

Planning Page

Summary

Write a brief summary of what you are going to write about.

Supporting Details

Write down the facts, details, or examples you are going to include in your answer.

Outline

Write a plan for what you are going to write. Include the main points you want to cover and the order you will cover them.

Responding to Literature – Writing Task 2

Directions: Read the passage below. Then answer the question that follows.

A New Start

Dear Diary,

What a day! I started at my new school this morning and had the best time. I made lots of new friends and really liked my teachers. I was so nervous the night before, but I had no reason to be. I was really worried that people might be mean to me, or just ignore me. I thought I might feel like an outsider. But everyone was friendly and polite. They made me feel at ease. It was like I'd been at the school for a hundred years!

The day started very early at 7:00 am. I had my breakfast downstairs with my mom. She could tell that I was very anxious. Mom kept asking me what was wrong. I think she knew that I was nervous about starting at a new school. She told me I had nothing to worry about and that everyone was going to love me. If they didn't love me, Mom said to send them her way for a good talking to. I couldn't stop laughing.

My mom dropped me off at the school gates about ten minutes before the bell. A little blonde girl got dropped off at the same time and started waving at me. She ran over and told me her name was Abigail. She was very nice and we became close straight away. We spent all morning together and began to chat to another girl called Stacey. Abigail and Stacey gave me a tour of the school. They showed me where my locker was, and showed me where they usually ate lunch together. They answered a lot of questions I had, and I started to feel a lot more relaxed.

The three of us sat together in class all day and we even made our way home together! Abigail told me that she would introduce me to some other people the next day. She invited me to a party the next week, and asked me if I wanted to join the tennis team with her.

The classes went very quickly as well. Luckily, there wasn't too much work to be done on the first day. I was also relieved that the teacher didn't make me stand in front of the class and introduce myself! That would have been embarrassing. My new teacher gave us a lot of information about what we would learn that year, but that's about it.

It is late now so I am going to sleep, but I cannot wait until tomorrow! I feel as though I am really going to enjoy my time at my new school. I only hope that my new friends feel the same way too.

Casey

1 How is Casey's day different from what she expected? Use details from the passage to support your answer.

In your answer, be sure to
- describe how Casey's day is different from what she expected
- use details from the passage in your answer
- write an answer of between 1 and 2 pages

Hint

The key to receiving full marks for this question is to support your answer well. You can start by writing about what Casey expected the day to be like. Use details from the letter to describe what Casey was worried about. Then describe how the day actually turned out. Use the details that Casey gives to describe her day. Finally, end your answer with a conclusion. The conclusion should be a 1-paragraph summary of the main ways her day was different than expected.

Planning Page

Summary

Write a brief summary of what you are going to write about.

Supporting Details

Write down the facts, details, or examples you are going to include in your answer.

Outline

Write a plan for what you are going to write. Include the main points you want to cover and the order you will cover them.

Responding to Literature – Writing Task 3

Directions: Read the passage below. Then answer the question that follows.

Gemma's Secret

Nobody knew that Gemma had a secret. Not even her older sister or her parents had the slightest idea. She had never told anyone, as she didn't think that they would understand. Everyone knew that Gemma was creative and imaginative. They also knew that she was a very shy and quiet young girl. What they didn't know is that Gemma's best friend was imaginary. They had been friends for more than two years. Her name was Taylor and she was the very best friend that a young girl could hope for.

Gemma and Taylor would often play together. Taylor followed Gemma like a shadow. They would chase each other in the park. They also liked to play with Gemma's collection of dolls in the back garden.

At night they whispered to each other and shared stories until Gemma drifted off to sleep. Even when Gemma was in the company of other friends, she would always think about Taylor. They were always together and sharing jokes between themselves.

One day Taylor just disappeared. Gemma was very upset that her friend was not around anymore. She looked everywhere for her, but she was nowhere to be found. She couldn't even tell her family why she was so sad because they had no idea Taylor existed.

For a while, Gemma was very quiet and didn't speak very much to anyone. It was only over time that she came to terms with her loss. She made new friends and grew even closer to her sisters.

Losing Taylor made Gemma appreciate her family and loved ones even more. She always remembered Taylor though and all the fun that she brought into her life.

1   Do you think that Gemma having an imaginary friend was good for her? Explain why or why not.

In your answer, be sure to
- give your opinion on whether or not having an imaginary friend was good for Gemma
- explain why you believe this
- use details from the passage in your answer
- write an answer of between 1 and 2 pages

Hint

This question is asking for your personal opinion. You can decide for yourself whether or not you think the imaginary friend was a good thing. You will not be marked based on which opinion you hold. Instead, you will be marked on how well you explain your opinion and support it with details from the passage. To start, first decide whether you think the imaginary friend was good for her or not. Then think of 2 or 3 reasons why you think this. In your answer, you should clearly describe these reasons. For each reason, you should use details from the passage.

Planning Page

Summary
Write a brief summary of what you are going to write about.

Supporting Details
Write down the facts, details, or examples you are going to include in your answer.

Outline
Write a plan for what you are going to write. Include the main points you want to cover and the order you will cover them.

Responding to Literature – Writing Task 4

Directions: Read the passage below. Then answer the question that follows.

Trying Too Hard

 Robert was determined to do well in his exams. He devoted all of his spare time to study. He had always wanted to be a lawyer when he grew up. He wanted to go to a good college and enjoy a successful career. Unfortunately, this meant that he was almost always serious.

Even though he was young, he was unable to relax and enjoy himself most of the time. His friends often got frustrated that he didn't want to spend much time with them.

Robert had an important exam due the following day. He had spent almost an entire week preparing for it. He had managed to get little sleep and was very tired. He even spent the night before the exam revising and had barely managed any sleep at all. However, he thought that he was ready for the exam. He was confident that he had worked harder than anyone else and was sure to get a perfect grade.

After Robert ate his breakfast, he started to feel a little ill. He was tired and unable to focus. He also had a small headache and found it very difficult to concentrate. He still refused to believe that he could ever fail the exam. Robert arrived at the school hall and took his seat beside his friends. He noticed how relaxed and happy they looked compared to him.

"They are just underprepared," he thought to himself as he began his paper.

Despite his best efforts, Robert wasn't able to finish his exam. After twenty minutes, he felt very hot and uncomfortable. He then slumped in his chair, and one of his friends called for help. The school doctor suggested that he was exhausted and would be unable to complete the exam.

He spent the lunch break in the nurse's office. He looked out the window and watched his friends. They smiled and joked and seemed to have not a care in the world. Robert decided that from then on, he wouldn't take it all so seriously.

"I guess I will know better next time," he mumbled.

1   The passage describes a boy who takes things too seriously. Think of a time when you took something too seriously. Describe that time and how it is similar to Robert's experience.

In your answer, be sure to

- describe a time when you took something too seriously
- describe how your situation was similar to Robert's experience
- use details from the passage in your answer
- write an answer of between 1 and 2 pages

Hint

The question asks you to relate to the passage. You have to write about your own experience of taking something too seriously. You will mainly use your own experience in your essay. You should describe what you took seriously and what happened. Be sure to provide enough details so the reader knows what happened. Then relate your experience to Robert's. You might describe how you both learned not to be so serious, or how things worked out poorly for you just like they did for Robert.

Planning Page

Summary
Write a brief summary of what you are going to write about.

Supporting Details
Write down the facts, details, or examples you are going to include in your answer.

Outline
Write a plan for what you are going to write. Include the main points you want to cover and the order you will cover them.

Responding to Literature – Writing Task 5

Directions: Read the passage below. Then answer the question that follows.

Happy Campers Summer Retreat

As a parent, your child's happiness is the most important thing to you. It is important to keep children healthy and active. This can be difficult to achieve. After all, many people have busy careers as well. The Happy Campers Summer Retreat was developed to help parents with this challenge.

Michael Gibson founded our group in 1998. We run a summer camp for children during the holidays. We are open from May to September. We look after lots of children every single year. The camp is based in the Colorado Mountains. It offers a wide range of activities for children. Our group's mission is to create a new generation of active children across America.

Our program helps improve:
- Physical fitness
- Problem-solving skills
- Social skills
- Sports ability and experience

The Happy Campers Summer Retreat can benefit all children. Some children are good at school, but rarely active. Our program will help encourage an interest in sports. Other children are mainly interested in sports. These children will play sports, but will also learn new skills. Team sports are also very important. They are used to help children develop teamwork skills, social skills, and communication skills. Children will also have the chance to try new activities. Our program is designed to help develop a complete and fully active child.

Our program is very affordable. It is available to any family in America. Your child's stay can be as short as a week or as long as six weeks. We will also cater to any special needs that your child may have.

Why not call us today or send us an email with your enquiry? Take action now and give your child this great opportunity! Our helpful staff will be able to give you all of the answers that you need.

1   What are the main benefits of the Happy Campers Summer Retreat? If you attended the retreat, which benefit do you think would be most important to you? Use details from the passage in your answer.

In your answer, be sure to
- describe the main benefits of the Happy Campers Summer Retreat
- describe which benefit would be most important to you
- use details from the passage in your answer
- write an answer of between 1 and 2 pages

Hint

There are two parts to this writing task. You should start by describing what the main benefits of the retreat are. Use the information in the passage to explain what the main benefits are. You should then write about how one benefit relates to you. Choose one benefit that you think would be most important to you. Write a paragraph or two describing why you choose this benefit or how this benefit would help you personally.

Planning Page

Summary
Write a brief summary of what you are going to write about.

Supporting Details
Write down the facts, details, or examples you are going to include in your answer.

Outline
Write a plan for what you are going to write. Include the main points you want to cover and the order you will cover them.

Part 3
Guided Writing Tasks

INTRODUCTION
For Parents, Teachers, and Tutors

Writing Skills

Students in grade 6 develop writing skills by producing writing for different purposes. There are three main writing purposes covered in grade 6:

- Writing to entertain – students write fictional stories based on a writing prompt
- Writing to describe – students write a personal narrative describing an experience
- Writing to explain or persuade – students write an essay giving their opinion on a topic or persuading someone to do something or agree with something

Part 3 of this book has one section for each type of writing. In each section, five writing prompts are provided.

Planning

Planning is the key to having students produce writing that is clear, focused, and effective. For each writing task, students should follow the instructions for planning their writing and complete the planning page before they start writing. Students should then write a composition of between 1 and 2 pages.

Hints

Each writing task includes a hint. Each hint is designed to have students focus on one area that will help them achieve good results in written tasks. After completing all five tasks, students will have developed key skills that will help ensure they score well on future writing tasks.

Preparing for the STAAR Writing Test

The STAAR Writing test taken by grade 7 students contains two writing prompts. One of the writing prompts requires students to write a personal narrative on a set topic. The writing tasks in the "Writing to Describe" section will help prepare students for this writing prompt. The second writing prompt on the state test requires students to produce expository writing, which is writing that communicates ideas or information. The writing tasks in the "Writing to Explain or Persuade" section will help prepare students for this writing prompt.

Writing to Entertain

About the Writing Tasks

In these writing tasks, you are asked to write a story. Each writing task gives you a writing prompt to use as the starting point of your story.

You should write a complete story with a beginning, middle, and end based on the writing prompt.

Plan Your Writing

Good writers plan their stories before they start writing. Follow the steps below to plan your story.

Step 1
Read the writing prompt and think of an idea for your story. Once you have decided what your story is going to be about, fill in the first box. You should describe what your story is going to be about.

Step 2
Fill in the second box by describing what is going to happen at the start of your story. At the start of the story, you might want to describe the main character and the main problem.

Step 3
Fill in the third box by describing what is going to happen in the middle of your story. In the middle of a story, a problem might get worse or a key event might occur.

Step 4
Fill in the fourth box by describing what is going to happen at the end of your story. The ending should solve the main problem.

Step 5
Start writing! Follow your plan as you write.

Step 6
After you have finished, check your work. Check your work for spelling, grammar, punctuation, and capitalization.

Writing to Entertain – Writing Task 1

Shane walked into the classroom and took his seat. Then Miss Marvin walked in. She was the strangest teacher that Shane had ever seen. And she was about to teach the strangest class ever.

Write a story about the class that Miss Marvin teaches.

Hint

The writing prompt tells you that your story should be about the class that Miss Marvin teaches, and it tells you that the class should be strange. Use this as the starting point and think of a story based around this idea. You can decide what is strange about the class. Use your imagination and come up with a clear idea about what happens that is strange. Then use your story to describe what happens. Be creative and try to make your story interesting!

Planning Page

The Story
Write a summary of your story.

The Beginning
Describe what is going to happen at the start of your story.

The Middle
Describe what is going to happen in the middle of your story.

The End
Describe what is going to happen at the end of your story.

Writing to Entertain – Writing Task 2

Joel was excited about moving into his new house. He really wanted to meet his new neighbors. He had seen kids about his age. They looked like they would be lots of fun.

Write a story about what happens when Joel meets his neighbors.

Hint

A good story has a beginning, middle, and end. As you plan your story, focus on what is going to happen in each part. The beginning often introduces the characters, the setting, and the main problem. The start of this story might describe when Joel first meets his neighbors. The middle of the story might describe what the neighbors are like, what happens when they meet, or something that goes wrong. This will be the main part of your story. It will usually be 2 or 3 paragraphs long. In this part, describe the events that take place. At the end of the story, there is usually some sort of resolution. If something has gone wrong, it might be solved at this point. If Joel has learned something from his neighbors, this part might describe how he has changed. This ties up the story and makes it a complete story.

Planning Page

The Story

Write a summary of your story.

The Beginning

Describe what is going to happen at the start of your story.

The Middle

Describe what is going to happen in the middle of your story.

The End

Describe what is going to happen at the end of your story.

Writing to Entertain – Writing Task 3

Look at the picture below.

Write a story based on what is happening in the picture.

Hint

Your story should be based on the picture given. You should use the picture to come up with an idea for your story. The story shows a boy who is trying to start a fire. Think about why the boy might be doing this. Is he lost? Does he live alone in the woods? Is he at a camp? A good story will often be based around a main problem that a character overcomes. Focus on thinking of what the character's main problem is, and develop a complete story based on solving this problem.

Planning Page

The Story
Write a summary of your story.

The Beginning
Describe what is going to happen at the start of your story.

The Middle
Describe what is going to happen in the middle of your story.

The End
Describe what is going to happen at the end of your story.

Writing to Entertain – Writing Task 4

Look at the picture below.

Write a story based on what is happening in the picture.

Hint

The setting of your story does not have to be the present. The picture suggests that this story could be set long ago. Use your imagination to think of an interesting story that could take place in an earlier time. Try to make sure all the details fit with the setting. For example, if your story has dialogue, try and write it how you imagine people might have spoken long ago.

Planning Page

The Story
Write a summary of your story.

The Beginning
Describe what is going to happen at the start of your story.

The Middle
Describe what is going to happen in the middle of your story.

The End
Describe what is going to happen at the end of your story.

Writing to Entertain – Writing Task 5

Karen was ready to step out onto the stage. She was trying out for the school play. She really wanted to get a good part in the play.

Write a story about Karen and how she tries out for the school play.

Hint

One way to improve your writing is to focus on how you describe things. You can choose words and phrases that make your writing more interesting. Imagine that you want to describe how nervous Karen felt before trying out. Instead of saying that she was nervous, you might describe how she paced back and forth.

You can also use literary devices such as similes or hyperbole to add emphasis. For example, you could write that Karen paced back and forth so many times that she started to wear a hole in the stage. By describing things in a more interesting way, you will make your story more interesting to the reader.

Planning Page

The Story
Write a summary of your story.

The Beginning
Describe what is going to happen at the start of your story.

The Middle
Describe what is going to happen in the middle of your story.

The End
Describe what is going to happen at the end of your story.

Writing to Describe

About the Writing Tasks

In these writing tasks, you are asked to describe a personal experience. Each writing task will give you a topic. You then have to write about a personal experience on that topic.

In these tasks, you can use your own opinion. You can write about what happened, how you felt, or what you think about something now.

Plan Your Writing

Before you start writing, plan what you are going to write. Follow the steps below to plan your writing.

Step 1

Start by thinking about the topic. Think about a time you could write about. You might think of several ideas. Choose one of these ideas to write about.

Step 2

Fill in the first box by writing a short summary of what you are going to write about.

Step 3

Fill in the second box by writing a plan of what you are going to write. Write down the main points you want to make, and the order you are going to cover them.

Step 4

Start writing! Follow your plan as you write.

Step 5

After you have finished, check your work. Check your work for spelling, grammar, punctuation, and capitalization.

Writing to Describe – Writing Task 1

Everyone needs help sometimes. Think about a time when you needed help. Who did you ask for help and how did the person help you?

Write a composition describing a time when you asked someone for help. Describe why you asked for help, who you asked for help, and what happened in the end.

Hint

Make sure you answer each part of the question. Remember that you need to include the following:

- why you asked for help
- who you asked for help
- what happened when you asked for help

When you write your outline, make sure that it covers all of the parts of the question.

Planning Page

Summary

Write a brief summary of what you are going to write about.

Outline

Write a plan for what you are going to write. Include the main points you want to cover and the order you will cover them.

Writing to Describe – Writing Task 2

It feels good to do something that you are proud of. Think about a time when you did something that you were proud of.

Write a composition describing a time when you did something that you were proud of. Explain what you did and why you felt proud.

Hint

Stay focused! You might be able to think of many different times you could write about, but don't try to write about them all. Instead, choose just one time and write about that time in detail. Your answer should describe what you did that you were proud of. You should include details that will help the reader imagine what you did and why you felt proud of it. When choosing which details to include, ask yourself whether the detail helps explain why you felt proud. For example, you might be proud because you achieved something that was difficult for you. It would then be relevant to explain why it was difficult for you.

Planning Page

Summary

Write a brief summary of what you are going to write about.

Outline

Write a plan for what you are going to write. Include the main points you want to cover and the order you will cover them.

Writing to Describe – Writing Task 3

Tiny Treasures

Tiny heart with a tiny beat,
Like the softness of a thousand tiny feet.
Smile that stretches far and wide,
My body feels warm and glows inside.
Just met my new baby sister today,
Now I wouldn't have life any other way.

The poet describes an important event for her family. Write a composition about an important event for your family. Describe the event and explain how you felt about it.

| Hint |

This writing task introduces the topic by using a poem. You do not have to refer to the poem in your answer. The poem is just there to help you start thinking about the topic. The goal of your writing is to write about an important event for your family. You should also clearly describe how you felt about the event. You could write about a positive event like a new baby being born like in the poem. Or you could write about a sad event. Whatever event you choose, be sure to explain how it made you feel and why.

Planning Page

Summary
Write a brief summary of what you are going to write about.

Outline
Write a plan for what you are going to write. Include the main points you want to cover and the order you will cover them.

Writing to Describe – Writing Task 4

Good friends and family members can sometimes have misunderstandings. Think about a time when you had a misunderstanding with a friend or family member.

Write a composition describing a misunderstanding that you had with a friend or family member. Describe what the misunderstanding was, what happened because of the misunderstanding, and what you think of the misunderstanding now.

Hint

When planning your writing, it is a good idea to break down what you want to say into paragraphs. This will help make sure your writing is well-organized and easy to understand. In your outline, describe what you are going to cover in each paragraph. For example, your outline could be something like this:

Introduction - what the misunderstanding was
Paragraph 1 - how the misunderstanding caused a fight
Paragraph 2 - how I realized that I was wrong
Paragraph 3 - how I fixed things by saying sorry
Conclusion - how I learned to listen to others and not always think that I am right

Planning Page

Summary

Write a brief summary of what you are going to write about.

Outline

Write a plan for what you are going to write. Include the main points you want to cover and the order you will cover them.

Writing to Describe – Writing Task 5

Do you share a room or do you have your own room? If you share a room, explain what the good and bad things are about sharing your room. If you have your own room, explain what the good and bad things are about having your own room.

Write a composition describing whether or not you share a room and what you like and dislike about it.

Hint

When writing compositions like this, you should focus on 2 or 3 things that you like and 2 or 3 things that you dislike. There may be many more things that you like and dislike. However, it is better to describe 2 or 3 things in detail than to write a long list of things without including any details or examples. You will be scored on how well you describe what you like and dislike, not on how many things you can think of! When you write your plan, choose the 2 or 3 things you like and dislike most and write one paragraph about each thing.

Planning Page

Summary

Write a brief summary of what you are going to write about.

Outline

Write a plan for what you are going to write. Include the main points you want to cover and the order you will cover them.

Writing to Explain or Persuade

About the Writing Tasks

In these writing tasks, you are asked to explain your opinion on a topic or to persuade someone to do something or believe something.

Each task will give you a topic to give your opinion on or a situation where you have to persuade someone to do something or believe something. You should use facts, details, or examples to support your opinion or argument.

Plan Your Writing

Before you start writing, plan what you are going to write.

Step 1
Start by thinking about the writing prompt. Think about what the purpose of your writing is. Focus on what you are trying to persuade someone to believe or do.

Step 2
Fill in the first box by writing the main purpose of your writing.

Step 3
Fill in the second box by listing the facts, details, or examples you are going to use to persuade the person.

Step 4
Fill in the third box by writing a plan of what you are going to write. Write down the main points you want to make, and the order you are going to cover them.

Step 5
Start writing! Follow your plan as you write.

Step 6
After you have finished, check your work. Check your work for spelling, grammar, punctuation, and capitalization.

Writing to Explain – Writing Task 1

Getting Things Done

I have a plan for tomorrow.
I have a plan for today.
As long as I stick to my plans,
nothing ever gets in my way.

In "Getting Things Done," the poet describes how he gets things done by planning. Do you think it is important to plan? Why or why not? Write a composition describing why it is important to plan, or why planning is unimportant.

Hint

You may have several different opinions. Maybe you think planning can sometimes be helpful, but that too much planning can make life boring. A good composition will have one clear idea. Even if you have several ideas, choose one to focus on in your writing. It is better to support one opinion very well than to describe many different opinions!

Planning Page

Summary

Write a brief summary of what you are going to write about.

Supporting Details

Write down the facts, details, or examples you are going to include.

Outline

Write a plan for what you are going to write. Include the main points you want to cover and the order you will cover them.

Writing to Persuade – Writing Task 2

Imagine that your cousin lives in another state. You want your cousin to come and stay at your home for a few weeks.

Write a letter to your cousin to persuade him or her to come and visit. Use reasons, facts, or details to persuade your cousin.

Hint

The writing prompt describes the purpose of your writing. In this case, you want to persuade someone to come and stay with you. You will need to give reasons that will help make your cousin want to stay with you. Think of two or three good reasons to use in your letter.

It is also important to think about who the audience is. This will impact the writing style that you use. You are writing this letter to your cousin. A letter to a cousin does not have to be formal or serious. You can write it in a casual way as if you are writing to a friend.

Planning Page

Summary

Write a brief summary of what you are going to write about.

Supporting Details

Write down the facts, details, or examples you are going to include.

Outline

Write a plan for what you are going to write. Include the main points you want to cover and the order you will cover them.

Writing to Persuade – Writing Task 3

Your school has decided that it wants a new mascot. Think of an animal that you think would make a good mascot.

Write an essay for your school newspaper. In the essay, you should persuade people to agree that the animal you have selected would make a good mascot. Use reasons, facts, or details in your essay.

Hint

The key to writing a good essay is to support it well! It does not matter what animal you choose. However, you should come up with reasons to support your choice. Make sure you describe these reasons in your essay.

The format and audience are also important to think about. This writing prompt asks for an essay instead of a letter. An essay should have more structure than a letter. It should have an introduction, a body, and a conclusion. The essay is also being written for the school newspaper. This audience would suit a more formal style than the letter you wrote to your cousin.

Planning Page

Summary
Write a brief summary of what you are going to write about.

Supporting Details
Write down the facts, details, or examples you are going to include.

Outline
Write a plan for what you are going to write. Include the main points you want to cover and the order you will cover them.

Writing to Explain – Writing Task 4

Read this proverb about work.

Many hands make light work.

Do you agree with this proverb? Explain why or why not. Use facts, details, or examples in your answer.

Hint

A proverb is a short saying that states an idea. The idea in this proverb is that many people make work easier. You have to explain whether or not you agree with this. When you are asked whether or not you agree with something, you will not be scored based on whether you agree or not. You will be scored on how well you explain why you do or do not agree. Don't worry about choosing the right answer. Instead, focus on what your personal opinion is. Then focus on clearly explaining why this is your opinion and giving reasons that will persuade other people to agree with you.

Planning Page

Summary
Write a brief summary of what you are going to write about.

Supporting Details
Write down the facts, details, or examples you are going to include.

Outline
Write a plan for what you are going to write. Include the main points you want to cover and the order you will cover them.

Writing to Explain – Writing Task 5

Read this piece of advice.

> If you can solve your problem, then what is the need of worrying? If you cannot solve it, then what is the use of worrying?
> -Shantideva

Do you think this is good advice? Explain why or why not.

Hint

Start by thinking about what the advice means. It means that there is no use worrying. Then think about whether you agree. Think about how this advice relates to your life. The advice can be applied to many areas. A good essay will be focused. Think about how it relates to one area of your life. It could be your studies, your friendships, or your goals. As you plan your writing, focus on this one area. This will help make sure you produce writing that has a clear and focused idea.

You can also use specific examples from your life to make your opinion clearer. For example, you could describe one situation where you worried a lot about something, and then write about how worrying did not help. To receive full marks, you can also expand on the topic and add your own advice. For example, you might argue that telling people not to worry is good advice. You could then add that people should take action to make things better.

Answer Key

Part 1: Reading and Writing Mini-Tests

Mini-Test 1

Mozart

Core Writing Skills Practice

Core skill: Write a research report

Answer: The student should write a complete research report. The research report should give key information about Ludwig van Beethoven. The report should be informative and should include facts and details. The report should be well-organized, well-written, and easy to understand.

Q1.

A complete answer should give two details that show that Mozart was gifted. Give a score of 0, 1, or 2 based on how many details are correctly given.

- The details may include that he composed over 600 pieces of music, that he wrote music for different instruments, that he wrote whole operas, or that he started composing music at age 5.

Q2.

A complete answer should complete the chart with the two places and the two details described below. Give a score of 0, 1, or 2 based on how many pairs of places and details are correctly listed.

- Paris   Searched for work / Wrote music
- Vienna   Wrote his best-known work

Clowns

Q1.
A complete answer should meet the criteria listed below. Give a score of 0, 1, or 2 based on how well the answer meets the criteria listed.

- It should identify Mickey's main problem as being that he is afraid of clowns.
- It should describe how he overcomes the problem by facing his fear.

Q2.
A complete answer should meet the criteria listed below. Give a score of 0, 1, or 2 based on how well the answer meets the criteria listed.

- It should identify that the word "pranced" indicates how the clowns moved.
- It should describe how the word "pranced" implies that the clowns moved in a joyful way.

Raindrops

Q1.
A complete answer should meet the criteria listed below. Give a score of 0, 1, or 2 based on how well the answer meets the criteria listed.

- It should describe how the diagram shows that raindrops are often shown as being shaped like tears.
- It may describe the diagram as an example of how weather reports often show raindrops.

Q2.
A complete answer should meet the criteria listed below. Give a score of 0, 1, or 2 based on how well the answer meets the criteria listed.

- It should compare the actual shape of raindrops with the mistaken shape of raindrops.
- It should describe how raindrops are spherical, but are mistaken as being teardrop-shaped.

Dearest Donna

Core Writing Skills Practice

Core skill: Write a poem

Answer: The student should write a poem of four lines where the second and fourth lines rhyme. The poem could be on any topic.

Q1.

A complete answer should meet the criteria listed below. Give a score of 0, 1, or 2 based on how well the answer meets the criteria listed.

- It may state that each verse has two pairs of rhyming lines.
- It may state that in each verse, lines 1 and 2 rhyme and lines 3 and 4 rhyme.

Q2.

A complete answer should meet the criteria listed below. Give a score of 0, 1, or 2 based on how well the answer meets the criteria listed.

- It should identify that the poem is addressed to Donna, or to the speaker's girlfriend.
- It should give evidence to support this. The evidence referred to could include the title of the poem, the use of "you" and "we" as showing that he is speaking to his girlfriend, or the message of the poem.

Penny's Powers

Core Writing Skills Practice

Core skill: Write an explanatory text

Answer: The student should describe a wish he or she would make. Students should clearly explain why they would make that wish.

Q1.
A complete answer should meet the criteria listed below. Give a score of 0, 1, or 2 based on how well the answer meets the criteria listed.

- It should give details that show that the events could not really happen.
- The answer should focus on how Penny has magic wishing powers that could not exist in real life.

Q2.
A complete answer should meet the criteria listed below. Give a score of 0, 1, or 2 based on how well the answer meets the criteria listed.

- It should identify the hyperbole as when the castle is described as almost reaching the clouds.
- It should identify the author's purpose as being to emphasize the height of the castle, or to create a sense of wonder.

Q3.
A complete answer should meet the criteria listed below. Give a score of 0, 1, 2, 3, or 4 based on how well the answer meets the criteria listed.

- It should explain that Penny realizes how lucky she is, or realizes that she can use her powers to help others.
- It should explain how Penny changes when she meets a homeless man. It should refer to how Penny sees the man's reactions to being given things, and how this makes her realize how lucky she is.
- It should use relevant details from the passage.
- It should be well-organized, clear, and easy to understand.

Mini-Test 2

Something Special

Core Writing Skills Practice

Core skill: Write a persuasive text

Answer: The student should write a letter from the point of view of Toby. The letter should be focused on persuading the coach to allow Toby to play. The letter should make valid arguments and make use of supporting details. The letter should be well organized, well-written, and easy to understand.

Q1.

A complete answer should complete the table with two ways that Toby keeps playing basketball from the passage. Give a score of 0, 1, or 2 based on how many correct ways are given.

- The ways include that he played on weekends with friends, that he played by himself after school, and that he practiced his ball skills.

Q2.

A complete answer should meet the criteria listed below. Give a score of 0, 1, or 2 based on how well the answer meets the criteria listed.

- It should explain that Toby improved his ball skills while practicing alone.
- It should describe how Toby's coach selected him because of his ball skills.

Brain Size

Core Writing Skills Practice
Core skill: Complete a short research project
Answer: The student should research how ants communicate with each other, and write a
short description of how ants communicate. The description should describe how
ants communicate using scent, and refer to the chemicals that ants secrete. The
description may also describe how ants communicate using sound.

Q1.
A complete answer should meet the criteria listed below. Give a score of 0, 1, or 2 based on
how well the answer meets the criteria listed.

- It should draw a conclusion about the author's purpose in using a question.
- It may describe how the author wants readers to think about the topic, or how the
author wants readers to be curious or interested.
- It may include a personal response on how the question affected the student.

Q2.
A complete answer should list two facts from the passage. Give a score of 0, 1, or 2 based on
how many facts are listed.

- The facts may include that the common ant has the largest brain size in relation to
its size, that the brain of an ant is 6 percent of body weight, that the brain of a
human is 2 percent of body weight, or how an average nest has 40,000 ants.

Mosquitoes

Core Writing Skills Practice
Core skill: Complete a short research project
Answer: The student should research and list diseases caused by mosquitoes. The diseases listed could include West Nile virus, Dengue fever, Yellow fever, Ross River fever, and St. Louis Encephalitis.

Q1.
A complete answer should meet the criteria listed below. Give a score of 0, 1, or 2 based on how well the answer meets the criteria listed.

- It should make a reasonable prediction of what another sentence would describe.
- The prediction should relate to Patrick Manson's research. For example, a reasonable prediction would be that the next sentence would describe what Patrick Manson learned about mosquitoes, or the impact his findings had.

Q2.
A complete answer should meet the criteria listed below. Give a score of 0, 1, or 2 based on how well the answer meets the criteria listed.

- It should identify one similarity between male and female mosquitoes. The similarity should be one mentioned in the passage, such as that both male and female mosquitoes carry diseases.
- It should identify one difference between male and female mosquitoes. The difference should be one mentioned in the passage, such as that only female mosquitoes bite humans or that male mosquitoes do not pass on diseases.

The Olympics

Core Writing Skills Practice

Core skill: Write a research report

Answer: The student should write a complete research report. The research report should give key information about one of the athletes chosen. The report should be informative and should include facts and details. The report should be well-organized, well-written, and easy to understand.

Q1.

A complete answer should list one fact and one opinion from the passage. Give a score of 0, 1, or 2 based on how many facts or opinions are correctly listed.

- The facts listed could include that the Olympics are global, that they feature indoor or outdoor sports, that there are summer and winter versions, that they are held every 4 years, that they were first held in 1896, or that London is the host of the 2012 Olympics.
- The opinions listed could include that they are enjoyed by people all over the world, that they are an important event, or that they bring people from all countries together.

Q2.

A complete answer should meet the criteria listed below. Give a score of 0, 1, or 2 based on how well the answer meets the criteria listed.

- It should give a personal opinion on why the Olympics are popular.
- The personal opinion should be fully explained.
- It may include supporting details, or may be based on the student's own ideas or experiences.

The Light

Core Writing Skills Practice

Core skill: Understand point of view

Answer: The student should write a paragraph or two describing the events from Christopher's point of view.

Q1.
A complete answer should meet the criteria listed below. Give a score of 0, 1, or 2 based on how well the answer meets the criteria listed.

- It should refer to how the author describes the light.
- It may refer to the light being described as "bright and dazzling" or how Christopher shields his eyes from it.

Q2.
A complete answer should meet the criteria listed below. Give a score of 0, 1, or 2 based on how well the answer meets the criteria listed.

- It should state whether Christopher feels afraid or curious. Either answer is acceptable, as long as students clearly explain why they have drawn this conclusion.
- It should include an explanation to support the opinion.

Q3.
A complete answer should meet the criteria listed below. Give a score of 0, 1, 2, 3, or 4 based on how well the answer meets the criteria listed.

- It should draw a valid conclusion about what the light is. The conclusion is likely to be that the light is from a spaceship or alien spacecraft, but other reasonable answers that are supported by the passage can also be accepted.
- It should make a valid prediction about what will happen next.
- It should be well-organized, clear, and easy to understand.

Mini-Test 3

Peace and Not War

Core Writing Skills Practice

Core skill: Write a personal narrative

Answer: The student should describe an argument he or she had with something. The answer should include who was argued with and what was argued about.

Q1.

A complete answer should meet the criteria listed below. Give a score of 0, 1, or 2 based on how well the answer meets the criteria listed.

- It should explain that Terry and Mark both want to watch different things on the television.
- It may specify that Mark hates football, while Terry hates cartoons.

Q2.

A complete answer should meet the criteria listed below. Give a score of 0, 1, or 2 based on how well the answer meets the criteria listed.

- It should explain that the lounge room sounding like a zoo shows how loud and chaotic it sounded.
- It may expand on this to suggest that describing the lounge room this way suggests that Terry and Mark were acting like animals.

The Dodo

Core Writing Skills Practice

Core skill: Write a research report

Answer: The student should write a complete research report. The research report should give information about why one of the animals on the list became extinct. The report should be informative and should include facts and details. The report should be well-organized, well-written, and easy to understand.

Q1.

A complete answer should meet the criteria listed below. Give a score of 0, 1, or 2 based on how well the answer meets the criteria listed.

- It should identify that the common phrase is "as dead as a dodo."
- It should explain that the phrase means that something is gone forever.

Q2.

A complete answer should list two reasons that dodos became extinct. Give a score of 0, 1, or 2 based on how many correct reasons are given.

- The reasons listed could include that dodos build their nests on the ground, that ground-based animals ate the eggs, that people hunted dodos for meat, and that forest habitats were destroyed.

Letter to the Editor

Core Writing Skills Practice

Core skill: Write an opinion piece

Answer: The student should write a paragraph giving an opinion on how the problems in the town park could be solved. The solutions should be relevant, reasonable, and clearly explained.

Q1.

A complete answer should complete the web with two examples of trash from the passage. Give a score of 0, 1, or 2 based on how many examples are correctly given.

- The examples should be cans and broken glass.

Q2.

A complete answer should meet the criteria listed below. Give a score of 0, 1, or 2 based on how well the answer meets the criteria listed.

- It should explain how Evan could improve his argument.
- It may describe how Evan could give more details, how Evan could use imagery, how Evan could compare the park to how it once was, or any other reasonable method for making the state of the park clearer to the reader.

Tom's Time Machine

Core Writing Skills Practice

Core skill: Write a short story

Answer: The student should write a short story about a journey into the past or future. The short story should be well-organized and well-written.

Q1.

A complete answer should meet the criteria listed below. Give a score of 0, 1, or 2 based on how well the answer meets the criteria listed.

- It should circle one of the words. Any of the words could be reasonable answers, as long as the choice is supported.
- It should include a reasonable and well-supported explanation of why the student chose that word.

Q2.

A complete answer should meet the criteria listed below. Give a score of 0, 1, or 2 based on how well the answer meets the criteria listed.

- It should identify the genre as science fiction.
- It should give relevant evidence. The evidence could be specific, such as stating that the passage involves time travel. The evidence could be general, such as stating that the passage involves things that are not possible now and that it involves science.

Creature Comforts

Core Writing Skills Practice

Core skill: Write an opinion piece

Answer: The student should give an opinion on whether or not he or she would enjoy being a farmer, and should support the opinion with a valid explanation.

Q1.
A complete answer should meet the criteria listed below. Give a score of 0, 1, or 2 based on how well the answer meets the criteria listed.

- It should identify that the theme is about caring for animals, living a simple life, or enjoying what you do.

Q2.
A complete answer should meet the criteria listed below. Give a score of 0, 1, or 2 based on how well the answer meets the criteria listed.

- It should identify that the personification used is where the wind is described as trying to annoy Fred.
- It should draw a valid conclusion about the purpose of the personification. The purpose could be to make the wind seem real, or to suggest that Fred was battling the elements.

Q3.
A complete answer should meet the criteria listed below. Give a score of 0, 1, 2, 3, or 4 based on how well the answer meets the criteria listed.

- It should make a valid inference about what matters most to Fred.
- It should refer to how Fred cares about taking care of his farm and animals.
- It should use relevant supporting details from the passage.
- It should be well-organized, clear, and easy to understand.

Mini-Test 4

Sugar

Core Writing Skills Practice
Core skill: Write a functional piece
Answer: The student should write a recipe for making one of the desserts listed. The recipe should clearly describe the steps in order.

Q1.
A complete answer should meet the criteria listed below. Give a score of 0, 1, or 2 based on how well the answer meets the criteria listed.

- It should list two facts or details about sugar given in the passage.
- The information should be paraphrased and not written exactly as stated in the passage.

Q2.
A complete answer should meet the criteria listed below. Give a score of 0, 1, or 2 based on how well the answer meets the criteria listed.

- It should describe how sugar should be heated without water, and how this makes it melt or caramelize.

Herbal Tea

Core Writing Skills Practice

Core skill: Complete a short research project

Answer: The student should complete the chart with one benefit of peppermint tea and one benefit of chamomile tea. Benefits of peppermint tea include aiding digestion, relieving headaches, and treating colds. Benefits of chamomile tea include reducing stress and helping people sleep.

Q1.

A complete answer should meet the criteria listed below. Give a score of 0, 1, or 2 based on how well the answer meets the criteria listed.

- It should explain that the main purpose of the passage is to instruct or to teach readers how to do something.

Q2.

A complete answer should list two actions that are optional. Give a score of 0, 1, or 2 based on how many correct actions are listed.

- The optional actions include adding sugar, letting the tea sit for longer than 30 seconds, and adding milk or cream.

A Day in the Life

Core Writing Skills Practice

Core skill: Write a short story

Answer: The student should write a short story about an exciting event that happens to a police officer.

Q1.

A complete answer should complete the chart with four activities mentioned in the passage. Give a score of 0, 1, or 2 based on how many activities are correctly listed.

- The activities listed should be doing paperwork, pulling over speeding people, tracking down thieves, and directing traffic.

Q2.

A complete answer should meet the criteria listed below. Give a score of 0, 1, or 2 based on how well the answer meets the criteria listed.

- It should clearly explain the relevance of the passage's title.
- It should refer to how the passage describes what a police officer does on a day at work.

Silver

Q1.

A complete answer should meet the criteria listed below. Give a score of 0, 1, or 2 based on how well the answer meets the criteria listed.

- It should explain that the table gives specific information on how much silver is used for different purposes.

Q2.

A complete answer should meet the criteria listed below. Give a score of 0, 1, or 2 based on how well the answer meets the criteria listed.

- It should explain that silver is not used because it is too expensive, or that copper is used instead because it is much cheaper.

Camels

Core Writing Skills Practice

Core skill: Write a research report

Answer: The student should write a complete research report. The research report should give information about how one of the animals or plants listed survives in the desert. The report should be informative and should include facts and details. The report should be well-organized, well-written, and easy to understand.

Q1.

A complete answer should meet the criteria listed below. Give a score of 0, 1, or 2 based on how well the answer meets the criteria listed.

- It should explain how a camel's hump helps it survive.
- It should refer to how a camel's hump stores fat, and how the camel can use the fat for energy.

Q2.

A complete answer should meet the criteria listed below. Give a score of 0, 1, or 2 based on how well the answer meets the criteria listed.

- It should identify details from the passage that the student found interesting.
- It should include a brief explanation of why the student found the details interesting.

Q3.

A complete answer should meet the criteria listed below. Give a score of 0, 1, 2, 3, or 4 based on how well the answer meets the criteria listed.

- It should describe some features of camels that help them survive in deserts.
- It should refer to how a camel's hump stores fat that can be used for energy.
- It may also describe how camels can store water in their bodies and blood, or how camels can take in a lot of water and then go for days without drinking.
- It should be well-organized, clear, and easy to understand.

Part 2: Responding to Literature

Score each writing task by giving the student a score out of 5 for each of the following criteria:

- Content and organization
- Word usage
- Sentence construction
- Mechanics

Add the scores to give a final score out of 20.

After scoring the writing task, review with students areas where they have scored well and areas where the scores could be improved. Give students guidance on what to focus on in the next writing task to improve their score.

	Task 1	Task 2	Task 3	Task 4	Task 5
Content and Organization To receive a full score, the response will: • answer all parts of the question • use relevant details from the passage • have well-developed ideas • have good transitions between ideas • be clear and easy to understand					
Word Usage To receive a full score, the response will: • use correct verb tense • have correct subject-verb agreement • use pronouns correctly • use words with the correct meaning • use a variety of words					
Sentence Construction To receive a full score, the response will: • use a variety of sentence structures • construct sentences correctly					
Mechanics To receive a full score, the response will: • have few or no spelling errors • have few or no grammar errors • have few or no capitalization errors • have few or no punctuation errors					
Total Score					

Part 3: Guided Writing Tasks

Writing to Entertain

Score each writing task by giving the student a score out of 5 for each of the following criteria:

- Content and organization
- Word usage
- Sentence construction
- Mechanics

Add the scores to give a final score out of 20.

After scoring the writing task, review with students areas where they have scored well and areas where the scores could be improved. Give students guidance on what to focus on in the next writing task to improve their score.

	Task 1	Task 2	Task 3	Task 4	Task 5
Content and Organization To receive a full score, the response will: • have a beginning, middle, and end • have a clear focus • have well-developed ideas • have good transitions between ideas • be clear and easy to understand					
Word Usage To receive a full score, the response will: • use correct verb tense • have correct subject-verb agreement • use pronouns correctly • use words with the correct meaning • use a variety of words • show evidence of well-chosen words					
Sentence Construction To receive a full score, the response will: • use a variety of sentence structures • construct sentences correctly					
Mechanics To receive a full score, the response will: • have few or no spelling errors • have few or no grammar errors • have few or no capitalization errors • have few or no punctuation errors					
Total Score					

Writing to Describe

Score each writing task by giving the student a score out of 5 for each of the following criteria:

- Content and organization
- Word usage
- Sentence construction
- Mechanics

Add the scores to give a final score out of 20.

After scoring the writing task, review with students areas where they have scored well and areas where the scores could be improved. Give students guidance on what to focus on in the next writing task to improve their score.

	Task 1	Task 2	Task 3	Task 4	Task 5
Content and Organization To receive a full score, the response will: • have an opening and a closing • be focused • have well-developed ideas • have good transitions between ideas • be clear and easy to understand					
Word Usage To receive a full score, the response will: • use correct verb tense • have correct subject-verb agreement • use pronouns correctly • use words with the correct meaning					
Sentence Construction To receive a full score, the response will: • use a variety of sentence structures • construct sentences correctly					
Mechanics To receive a full score, the response will: • have few or no spelling errors • have few or no grammar errors • have few or no capitalization errors • have few or no punctuation errors					
Total Score					

Writing to Explain or Persuade

Score each writing task by giving the student a score out of 5 for each of the following criteria:

- Content and organization
- Word usage
- Sentence construction
- Mechanics

Add the scores to give a final score out of 20.

After scoring the writing task, review with students areas where they have scored well and areas where the scores could be improved. Give students guidance on what to focus on in the next writing task to improve their score.

	Task 1	Task 2	Task 3	Task 4	Task 5
Content and Organization To receive a full score, the response will: • have an opening and a closing • have a clear focus • have well-developed ideas • include strong arguments with supporting details • have good transitions between ideas • be clear and easy to understand • use supporting details					
Word Usage To receive a full score, the response will: • use correct verb tense • have correct subject-verb agreement • use pronouns correctly • use words with the correct meaning					
Sentence Construction To receive a full score, the response will: • use a variety of sentence structures • construct sentences correctly					
Mechanics To receive a full score, the response will: • have few or no spelling errors • have few or no grammar errors • have few or no capitalization errors • have few or no punctuation errors					
Total Score					

Texas Test Prep Reading Workbook

For additional reading test prep, get the Texas Test Prep Reading Workbook. It contains 40 reading mini-tests covering all the reading skills on the STAAR test. It is the perfect tool for ongoing test prep practice and for reading skills revision.

372.623 T355   HEI
Texas Test Prep writing workbook.

HEIGHTS
06/14

29567742R00083

Made in the USA
Charleston, SC
16 May 2014